Life in a Colony

Bees

Richard and Louise Spilsbury

www.heinemann.co.uk/library

To order:

☎ Phone 44 (0) 1865 888066
🖹 Send a fax to 44 (0) 1865 314091
🖥 Visit the Heinemann Bookshop at www.heinemann.co.uk/library to browse our catalogue and order online.

First published in Great Britain by Heinemann Library, Halley Court, Jordan Hill, Oxford OX2 8EJ, part of Harcourt Education.
Heinemann is a registered trademark of Harcourt Education Ltd.

© Harcourt Education Ltd 2004
The moral right of the proprietor has been asserted.

Editorial: Nicole Irving and Georga Godwin
Design: Ron Kamen and Celia Floyd
Picture Research: Rebecca Sodergren and
  Ginny Stroud-Lewis
Production: Viv Hichens

Originated by Dot Gradations Ltd
Printed in Hong Kong, China by Wing
  King Tong
ISBN 0 431 18268 X
08 07 06 05 04
10 9 8 7 6 5 4 3 2 1

British Library Cataloguing in Publication Data

Spilsbury, Richard and Spilsbury, Louise
Animal Groups: Bees – Life in a Colony
595.7'99156
A full catalogue record for this book is available from the British Library.

Acknowledgements

The Publishers would like to thank the following for permission to reproduce photographs:

Corbis/Treat Davidson/FLPA p. 28; FLPA/Minden Pictures/Konrad Wothe p. 17; FLPA/Ray Bird p. 11; FLPA/S. & D. & K. Maslowski p. 12; Nature Picture Library/David Shale p. 25 (bottom); Nature Picture Library/Dietmar Nill p. 9; Nature Picture Library/Jim Clare p. 5; Nature Picture Library/Lynn Stone p. 25 (top); Nature Picture Library/Pete Oxford p. 27; NHPA/Mark Bowler p. 4; NHPA/Stephen Dalton pp. 7, 19; Oxford Scientific Films pp. 15, 20, 22; Oxford Scientific Films/John Brown p. 26; Oxford Scientific Films/Lee Lyon, SAL p. 24; Oxford Scientific Films/Paulo De Oliveira p. 13; Ocford Scientific Films/Zebra Films Ltd/SAL p. 14; Oxford Scientific Films/Satoshi Kuribayashi pp. 18, 21; Oxford Scientific Films/Scott Camazine pp. 6, 10, 16.

Cover photograph of the group of bees, reproduced with permission of NHPA/Stephen Dalton.

The Publishers would like to thank Colin Fountain for his assistance in the preparation of this book.

Every effort has been made to contact copyright holders of any material reproduced in this book. Any omissions will be rectified in subsequent printings if notice is given to the Publishers.

Contents

What are bees? 4

What is a bee colony like? 6

How does a colony start? 9

What is a bee nest like? 12

How are honeycombs made? 15

What do bees eat? 17

How do bees communicate? 21

What dangers does a bee colony face? 24

How does a colony change? 27

Bee facts 29

Glossary 30

Find out more 31

Index 32

Any words appearing in the text in bold, **like this**, are explained in the Glossary.

What are bees?

Bees are a kind of **insect**. There are at least 25,000 **species** (different kinds) of bees in the world. The largest is the leaf-cutter bee, which measures almost 4 centimetres – about as long as your thumb. The smallest is the stingless bee of Brazil, which is only about 2 to 5 millimetres long. Most bees have black and yellow stripes, but some have red or orange patches or stripes and others are metallic green, blue or even red.

What is an insect?

Insects are small animals with a body in three sections: head, **thorax** and **abdomen**. Most insects have six legs and a pair of wings when adult. A hard shell-like skin called an exoskeleton protects their insides.

This is a buff-tailed bumblebee. A bee's eye is really many small eyes connected together. The **antennae** are used to smell. The **mandibles** are used for holding or cutting things.

antennae

eye

mandibles

Where do bees live?

Bees live in countries all over the world. They live in many different kinds of **habitat** from **tropical** forests to cool meadows, from city gardens to quiet leafy woodlands. The only places you will not find bees are at the freezing **Poles** and in the hottest deserts.

Which bees live in groups?

Most bee species live alone, except when it is time to **mate**. These are the solitary bees. Some kinds of bees are **social** insects that spend their whole lives in groups. Groups of bees are called colonies. In this book we look at some of these social bees and focus mainly on the two most well-known kinds – honeybees and bumblebees.

This is a large colony of wild honeybees.

What is a bee colony like?

Some colonies of bees are massive. Honeybee colonies can contain up to about 80,000 bees – bumblebees tend to form smaller groups. A colony of bees is like an enormous family where everyone helps and depends on each other. There are three main kinds of bee in most colonies – **workers**, **drones** and a **queen**. Each of the different kinds of bee has a particular job to do.

What does the queen do?

Most colonies have only one queen. The queen has just one job in life – to lay eggs every day. Whatever the size of the colony, she produces all of the colony's young. The queen is the mother of all the other bees. This means that all the bees in a colony are closely related.

The queen (centre) is the biggest, most important member of the colony. She can lay her own weight in eggs every day – that is about 1500 eggs!

What are drones?

Drones are the **male** bees in a colony. A drone's job is to **mate** with a queen so that she can begin to lay eggs and produce young. A small number of drones develop at certain times of the year. In large honeybee colonies a few hundred drones hatch in summer. Most drones do not live long. Once they have served their purpose, they die.

Worker bees

Worker bees are **females** that cannot lay eggs. Worker bees, as their name suggests, do all the work in the colony! They feed, clean and look after the queen. They make, tidy, repair and guard the nest that the colony lives in. They also look after the queen, the eggs and the young bees that hatch out of the eggs.

Workers are the smallest bees in a colony. Drones are bigger with large eyes.

worker

drone

Do worker bees share jobs?

A worker's jobs usually change as it gets older. At first, young adult workers feed **larvae**. When they are older they move on to building and mending the nest. Finally, they collect food for the colony.

How many bees are in a colony?

In an average honeybee colony in summer there might be 1 queen, 250 drones, 20,000 workers collecting food, 40,000 workers looking after the nest and young, 7000 eggs, 10,000 larvae and 20,000 **pupae**!

The life cycle of a honeybee

Honeybees begin life as eggs about the same size as a comma on this page. After four days they hatch into larvae that the workers feed. Almost a week later the larvae stop feeding and become pupae. During this stage they change into adults and after two weeks they are fully grown. Very few larvae become queens and drones – most become workers.

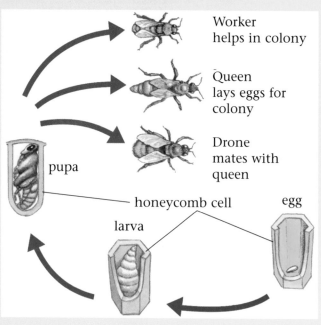

Worker helps in colony

Queen lays eggs for colony

Drone mates with queen

pupa

honeycomb cell

egg

larva

How does a colony start?

New bumblebee colonies begin each year, when a new **queen** starts to lay eggs. In autumn, all **workers**, **drones** and the old queen from an old bumblebee colony die. Only the new queen lives on.

In spring, a new bumblebee queen finds a safe place to nest. She makes a **wax** pot, like a thimble, and lays about six eggs in it. The queen feeds and protects the **larvae** that hatch out of these eggs. When this first set of bees are fully grown, they take over the work and the queen just lays more eggs. The workers enlarge the nest and feed and care for the queen and new larvae that hatch out. This happens again and again so the colony gets bigger and bigger.

These worker bumblebees are busy building a new nest.

When do honeybee colonies start?

Honeybee colonies can last for many years. New colonies of honeybees usually form when an old colony becomes too crowded. The old queen leaves with some of the workers and drones to start another colony. These groups of flying bees are called **swarms** and they usually form in hot weather.

Back in the old colony new queens are born. They fly out of the nest with some drones and **mate** in the air. One new queen will return to the original nest to lay eggs and take over the colony. The other queens go off to create new colonies elsewhere. If more than one queen returns to the original nest, the queen bees may fight until one becomes the new queen of the colony.

Honeybee swarms move together like a black cloud in the sky. When they land, they often form shapes like the one shown here.

Soon after new honeybee queens become adults they fly out of the nest. Drones flying out of the nest mate with the queens in the air. This is called a nuptial (wedding) flight.

What is a bee nest like?

Bees' nests come in many shapes and sizes. Some nests are the size of the palm of your hand; others can be as long as a small car!

Honeybees may make their nests tucked away inside trees or buildings, although they sometimes make them hanging from branches in the open. Bumblebees usually make nests in holes in the ground, for example in abandoned mouse burrows. A bee's nest is made up of many **cells**, which are like tiny little rooms, made out of **wax**. Bumblebee colonies build their wax cells inside balls of grass or moss. Their rounded, pot-shaped cells vary in size and shape. The cells in all bees' nests are used for young bees to develop in and to store food such as **honey**.

Bees usually make their nests in sheltered places, such as in old tree trunks.

Keeping safe

A bee's nest usually has one entrance hole with a platform outside for bees to land on. **Workers** guard this so pests like wax-eating caterpillars cannot get in. Nests also have a waterproof layer to keep the rain out. This is sometimes made of **resin**. This outer layer helps to hide the nest too. Carder bees, a kind of bumblebee, weave bits of moss together to hide their nest.

How do bees look after the nest?

Worker bees clean nests by removing faeces (poo), dirt and spilt food. Honeybees have a big spring-clean after resting in a nest through winter. Workers also mend any holes in the nest to keep out rain and cold air. They fill gaps with propolis, or bee's glue, which they collect from sticky buds of certain trees.

When carder bees cover their underground nest with moss they leave a single hole, through which they fly in and out.

13

What is a honeycomb?

A honeybee colony's nest is made of thousands of hexagonal (six-sided) cells that fit together neatly. These are arranged in upright sections. Each section is called a **honeycomb**. Sometimes honeycombs are protected by a nest wall. Bees move through passageways between the wall and the honeycomb.

Inside a honeycomb

Inside the nest, workers use some of the honeycomb cells for storing food. These cells are usually nearest the top. Below these are cells for the worker eggs and **larvae**. The **queen** lays one egg in each cell. Workers make larger cells on the edge of honeycombs for new queens and **drones** to develop in. The cells in a honeycomb always slope downwards from the top to the base. This stops things inside the cells from falling out.

This wild honeybee's nest is made up of seven honeycombs.

How are honeycombs made?

Bee colonies have to make the **wax** they use to build their nests. The first ingredients are flakes of fat made in their **abdomen**. They mix and chew these with saliva (spit) in their mouth. Different bees may mix other things in too, such as soil, **resin** or **pollen**.

Teamwork

A colony of bees can only build **honeycombs** because they work together. Teams of **worker** bees start off with a ring of wax at the top of the nest and build downwards. They do not build complete **cells** one by one. They make the sides of several cells next to each other at the same time.

How many cells do bees make?

Bee colonies usually make about six honeycombs inside a nest with a total of about 100,000 cells in them. It takes more than 2 kilograms of beeswax to make a set of honeycombs like this!

Bees use their **mandibles** and legs to shape the soft wax into the cells of their honeycomb.

Keeping the right temperature

Bees need to be at a steady temperature of 35 °C to make the fatty flakes they need for wax. This is also the temperature that **larvae** need to grow properly. If the nest gets too hot, teams of honeybee workers beat their wings at the nest entrance to blow in cool air. If the nest gets too cold, bees warm up by eating **honey** for **energy** and shaking their wings. They also huddle together for warmth.

These bees are beating their wings at the entrance of their nest to cool it down.

Mathematical builders

Honeybee workers measure each cell so that every one is exactly the right size. They test the size of each cell and the thickness of the cell walls using their antennae. Each cell wall of a honeycomb is usually 0.073 millimetres thick. If the wax is too thick in one spot, they scrape some off and use it elsewhere!

What do bees eat?

Bees get all the food they need from the flowers of many different kinds of plants. They take **pollen** and **nectar** from the centre of flowers. Pollen is high in **protein**, which animals need to build or repair body parts. Nectar gives bees sugars they need for **energy**.

How do bees find food?

The bees from a particular colony usually feed from just two types of flower. Bees may travel up to 1 mile (2 kilometres) from the colony's nest to find the right ones. Bees find flowers by looking out for their brightly coloured petals and smelling the sweet scents that the flowers give off.

Bees can fly well so that they can move quickly between many flowers. The hairs on a bumblebee's **thorax** help keep its wing muscles warm so that it can fly in cool weather.

17

Collecting food

Bees suck up nectar using their proboscis, which is a drinking straw-shaped tongue that curls up when not in use. Bees store the nectar in a special pouch called a honey stomach. Pollen from the flower sticks to a bee's hairy coat. The bee's legs brush this pollen into a ball and into its pollen baskets to carry it home. Pollen baskets are hairless patches on a bee's back legs surrounded by long hairs that form a basket shape!

Bees and flowers are a good example of the way plants and animals need each other to live.

What is pollination?

When bees visit flowers for food they also help to **pollinate** the flowering plants. When a bee crawls into a flower for nectar, some of the pollen attached to its body from a previous flower rubs off on the new one. The pollen fertilizes the second flower – it makes the flower produce seeds that can grow into new plants.

Do bees share food?

The **worker** bees that collect food for the colony return to the nest to share it with the bees working in the nest. They bring up the nectar from their honey stomach and pass it on by mouth. The bees in the nest eat some of this nectar and use some to make **honey**. Honeybees store honey for winter when the flowers of most plants have died off and there is less food about.

When a wax cell is full of honey, honeybees seal it with wax to keep it fresh, just as we seal things in a jar with a lid.

How do bees make honey?

To make honey, bees mix nectar with saliva in their mouths and put droplets of the mixture into a wax cell. They leave it here and fan it with their wings to let some of the water from the nectar **evaporate** into the air. The sticky substance that is left is the honey.

19

What do larvae eat?

Adult bees eat some of the pollen they collect, but they feed most of it to the colony's **larvae**. Protein foods are often called bodybuilders and bee larvae need protein-rich pollen to grow. When workers return to the nest with full pollen baskets they store pollen in cells. Other workers mix the pollen with nectar to form a mixture called beebread, which they feed to the larvae.

Worker bees feed larvae that are developing inside their wax cells.

What is royal jelly?

Royal jelly – or bee milk – is creamy-white and very rich in vitamins and protein. Worker bees make it by chewing pollen. They feed it to all larvae for the first two to three days of life. Larvae that will become **workers** or **drones** are then fed beebread, but those that will become **queen** bees continue to be fed royal jelly. This is because a queen needs lots of protein to be able to lay lots of eggs!

How do bees communicate?

Animals that live in groups need to be able to **communicate** with each other. They need to pass information to each other about many different things, such as what is going on in the group and where to find food. Bee colonies communicate mostly by smell and taste, but they also tell each other things by doing special dances!

Do bees use scent to communicate?

Bees in a colony recognize each other and their enemies by scents called **pheromones**. The **queen** makes the most important pheromones. When **workers** lick and clean her they pick up some of her scent and pass it on to the other bees. The smell and taste of it passes on information, such as what the queen needs. It also makes the whole colony share the same smell. This means that bees only need to smell another bee to know if it belongs to their colony or not.

When bees in a colony touch mouths to pass on food they share the colony smell.

Honeybee queens give off a particular pheromone to attract other bees to follow them to a new home when it is time to **swarm**. Worker bees also give off a particular pheromone to warn others of danger and call other workers to help them defend the colony.

In tropical stingless bees like these, workers leave trails of scent to lead other workers from their colony to food. Worker bees know they are getting closer to the food when the scent gets stronger.

Why do bees buzz?

You have probably heard bees buzzing and it may sound as if they are communicating. In fact buzzing is the sound made by the rapid beating of their wings. When a nest is disturbed, bees buzz more because they beat their wings faster to fan alarm scents through the colony. Honeybees can beat their wings over 11,000 times a minute!

Why do bees dance?

Worker bees from a honeybee colony are always on the lookout for new sources of food. When a worker bee finds one, it returns to the nest and performs a dance – a sequence of movements – on the side of the **honeycomb** to tell the others where the food source is.

Bees may dance in a circle shape, or in a shape like a number 8. The line the bee walks between the loops of the 8 tells the other bees how far to the left or right of the Sun they must go. The dancing bee waggles its **abdomen** to show how far away the flowers are. The faster the waggling, the closer the flowers are to the nest!

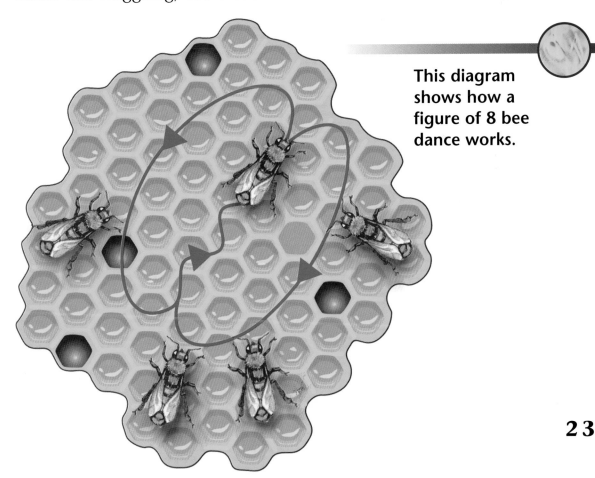

This diagram shows how a figure of 8 bee dance works.

What dangers does a bee colony face?

Some animals attack a bee colony to try to eat the **honey**, **larvae** and sometimes the **wax** inside. Bee **predators** include bears such as the sloth bear, skunks and a kind of bird called a bee-eater. Tiny **insects** called varroa mites bite bees and give them a disease, which has destroyed many wild honeybee colonies. People also harm bees when they spray **pesticides** and cut down trees and other places where they make nests.

The cleverest predator?

The honeyguide bird must get the prize for smartest bee predator. Its beak cannot break open a nest, so it leads ratels (honey badgers) to bees' nests. Once the nest is found and broken, the bird and the ratel take all they want to eat.

The ratel has tough claws that can open nests and it makes a smell that calms down the bees inside.

People who keep bees for their honey keep them in artificial nests called hives. Beekeepers have to wear protective clothing because when a bee colony is disturbed workers may fly out and attack.

In some countries, such as Nepal, honey hunters take honey from wild nests. They usually leave enough honey for the bee colony to survive.

How does a colony defend itself?

Most **queen** and **worker** bees have stingers they use to attack enemies. A bee's stinger is formed from a tube at the end of a bee's **abdomen**. A stinger pierces the skin of an animal and injects poison into it. If a honeybee stings a large animal, barbs (hooks) on the stinger hook into the skin and pull the bee's stinger out, killing the bee. This does not happen when the stinger is used on another insect.

What are killer bees?

Africanized honeybees are also called killer bees. These bees behave normally when hunting for food, but if they sense their colony is in danger they defend it angrily. If large numbers attack animals or people nearby they can kill because they deliver so many stings at once.

This is a killer bee. Angry killer bees may pursue animals for great distances to defend their colony.

26

How does a colony change?

Bumblebee colonies that live in places with cold winters change drastically each year. Almost all the bumblebees in the colony die off, because they do not store enough **honey** to survive winter when few flowers bloom. Only some young **queens** survive. They hibernate by going into a deep sleep underground or in a pile of leaves. They emerge again in spring to start a new colony.

Do honeybee colonies change?

Honeybee colonies change less drastically. By autumn many **workers** have died, because they only live for about six weeks in summer, the busiest time of year. Those born in late autumn stay with the colony. Any **drones** that are still around are not allowed back into the nest so they die too.

In autumn, remaining honey bees, workers and their queen huddle together in the nest and eat stored honey to survive the cold winter months.

What happens if a queen dies?

Honeybee colonies change in summer when **swarms** leave to form new colonies. They also change when a queen dies. A queen honeybee can live for about five years, but as she grows older she produces less **pheromone**. This acts as a message to tell workers to start feeding **royal jelly** to future queens and to prepare drones to **mate** with them. However, if a new queen tries to take over before the old queen is ready, the old queen kills her with her stinger!

Do new queens ever lead swarms?

In stingless bees, old queens become too fat to fly when the colony gets overcrowded. Young queens lead swarms away to form new colonies, taking honey, **pollen** and even **wax** with them too! The old queen stays behind in the old colony.

Bees in a colony know all about their queen from her scent. News about the queen can spread to every bee in a colony within fifteen minutes!

Bee facts

What does 'Busy as a bee' mean?

You have probably heard the phrase 'Busy as a bee' before, but have you thought about what it means? It refers to someone who is always busy doing something useful and compares him or her to the **worker** bees in a colony.

How far can bees fly?

Honeybees can fly up to 8 miles (14 kilometres) away from their nest when they go looking for food. Most of the time they only go 1 mile (up to 2 kilometres) in a single trip. Bees usually fly at about 9 miles (15 kilometres) an hour, but their top speed may be around 18 miles (30 kilometres) an hour!

Do bees help people?

Bees and bee products are incredibly useful to people. Bees **pollinate** most of the food plants in the world. **Honey** is a healthy food and is sometimes used to fight certain infections. Some people even eat **royal jelly** because it is thought to improve health.

Does honey always taste the same?

Honey can taste very different! The taste and colour of honey depends on the flowers the bees in a colony take their **nectar** from. For example, honey made from clover flowers looks and tastes different from honey made from fruit tree blossoms.

How much honey can bees make?

Honeybees have to collect **nectar** from over 5 million flowers to make just one kilogram of honey! In just one year a colony may collect more than 100 kilograms of nectar! With this they make more than 18 kilograms of honey to survive the winter.

Glossary

abdomen   third or lower section (soft belly) of an insect's body

antennae   pair of feelers on an insect's head

cells   tiny boxes to keep young or store honey and pollen in a honeycomb

communicate   pass on information to other animals

drone   male bee

energy   energy allows living things to live and grow

evaporate   turn from a liquid into a gas

female   animal that, when grown up, can become a mother

habitat   place where an animal or plant lives

honey   sweet syrup bees make for their food

honeycomb   group of hexagonal cells built of beeswax

insect   small six-legged animals that, when adult, have bodies divided into three sections

larvae   first stage in the life of insects that hatch out of eggs and look like little white grubs

male   animal that, when mature, can become a father

mandibles   jaws

mate/mating   when bees mate, a drone puts sperm inside a queen bee's body to fertilize the eggs inside her

nectar   sweet, sugary juice flowers make to attract bees

pesticides   sprays some farmers use to kill insects that feed on plants

pheromone   perfume-like substance

Poles   there are two Poles. The North Pole and the South Pole at the opposite ends of the Earth.

pollen   powder flowers make that can start seeds growing if they land in another flower

pollinate   when pollen moves from one flower to another

predators   animals that hunt or catch other animals to eat

protein   part of food that helps animals grow strong body parts

pupae   stage in growth just before an insect becomes an adult

queen   bee that lays all the eggs in a colony

resin   sticky substance some plants and trees make

royal jelly   milky food made by worker bees

social   animals that live in groups

species   group of living things that are similar and can reproduce together to produce healthy offspring

swarm   large group of insects that move while remaining very close together

thorax   middle part of an insect's body

tropical   area with some of the hottest temperatures in the world

vitamins   nutrients that keep an animal healthy

wax   substance bees use to make honeycombs

workers   female bees that do all the work in a bee colony

Find out more

Books

Oxford Reds: Bees Robert Dawson (Oxford University Press, 2000)

Questions and Answers About Bees, Betty Polisar Reigot (Scholastic, 1996)

Websites

At www.pbs.org/wgbh/nova/bees there is lots of information in 'Tales from a hive'.

You can go inside a hive for an animated, interactive exploration at www.pbs.org/wnet/nature/alienempire.

There are lots of amazing facts about bees and ideas for projects you can do at www.bees4kids.org.uk.

Index

antennae   4, 16

beebread   20
beekeepers   25
body parts   4
bumblebees   4, 5, 9, 12, 27
buzzing   22

carder bees   13
cells   12, 13, 14, 15, 16, 19, 20
colonies   5, 6, 7, 8, 9–10, 21, 25,
    27, 28
colours   4
communication   21–3, 28

dance   23
dangers   22, 24, 26
drones   6, 7, 8, 9, 10, 11, 14, 20,
    27, 28

eggs   6, 7, 8, 9, 10, 14, 20
energy   16, 17
eyes   4, 7

flowers   17, 18, 29
flying   10, 11, 17, 29
food   8, 12, 14, 17–20, 22, 23

habitats   5
hibernaton   27
hives   25
honey   12, 16, 19, 24, 25, 27, 28, 29
honeybees   5, 6, 7, 8, 10, 11, 12, 13,
    14, 16, 19, 22, 24, 26, 27, 28, 29
honeycombs   13, 14, 15, 23

insects   4, 24

killer bees   26

larvae   8, 9, 14, 16, 20, 24
life cycle   8

mandibles   4, 15
mating   5, 7, 10, 11, 28

nectar   17, 18, 19, 29
nest cleaning   14
nest repairing   14
nests   5, 7, 8, 9, 12-16, 19, 22, 25, 27
nuptial   11

pheromones   21, 22, 28
pollen   15, 17, 18, 20, 28
pollination   18, 29
predators   13, 24
proboscis   18
pupae   8

queens   6, 7, 8, 9, 10, 11, 14, 20, 21,
    22, 26, 27, 28

resin   13, 15
royal jelly   20, 28, 29

size   4
social insects   5
species of bees   4
stingers   26, 28
stingless bees   4, 22, 28
swarms   10, 22, 28

temperature   16

wax   9, 12, 15, 16, 19, 24, 28
wings   16, 22
worker bees   6, 7, 8, 9, 10, 13, 14, 15,
    16, 19, 20, 21, 22, 23, 26, 27, 29

Titles in the *Animal Groups* series include:

Hardback   0 431 18268 X

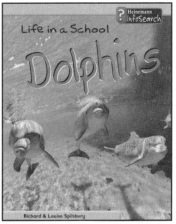

Hardback   0 431 18264 7

Hardback   0431 18267 1

Hardback   0 431 18265 5

Hardback   0 431 18269 8

Hardback   0 431 18266 3

Find out about the other titles in this series on our website www.heinemann.co.uk/library